TEACHING IN THE VUCA WORLD

DR DHEERAJ MEHROTRA

Copyright © Dr Dheeraj Mehrotra
All Rights Reserved.

Contents

Preface

VUCA is an abbreviation that arose out of the military during the 1990s. It portrays the "haze of war" — the turbulent conditions experienced in an advanced combat zone. Its importance to pioneers in business is evident, as these conditions elucidate the climate where the company is led each day. Authority, not surprisingly, including making a dream, isn't sufficient in a VUCA world. TEACHING IN THE VUCA WORLD, a priority on cards, fetches the world of uncertainties. The new world order of VOLATILE, UNCERTAIN, COMPLEX, and AMBIGUOUS approaches reflects new everyday learning and exploring the novel working order. The book Teaching in the VUCA World Explores the learning strategies of the new order!

Happy Learning!! Cheers! Connect via www.authordheerajmehrotra.com

Dr Dheeraj Mehrotra (Author)

I

Learning In the VUCA World

Out of nowhere, I went over this word VUCA, Volatile, Uncertain, Complex, and Ambiguous, distinguishing the new world request of range with no decision except for an approach to confronting the difficulties changing over them into favourable circumstances.

Without a doubt, the world is confronting a difficult time today. Nobody was at any point arranged for this and will at any moment be. The need we the people must have a deduction today towards having a bunch of essential abilities, information and demeanour, and business purchases these at a cost.

Understanding the VUCA World, the better! The abbreviation VUCA - Volatile, Uncertain, Complex, and Ambiguous - was authored during the 1990s. It depicts numerous individuals' experiences of their work environment incredibly well.

In this sort of climate, it tends to be challenging to feel like you are adapting - not to mention flourishing. The abbreviation VUCA - Volatile, Uncertain, Complex, and Ambiguous - was instituted during the 1990s. It depicts numerous individuals' experiences of their work environment amazingly well. In the learning environment, the learners, particularly the students, need to come back to a supportive, friendly atmosphere, where their learning loss and socio-emotional needs are recognised, dwelled, and curated as per the new world order and acknowledged by the educators at large. These notions and craftings are required to help them get back on track. Let us revisit the fact that one of the key lessons learnt throughout the crisis is the importance of engaging parents and communities in pupils' learning process. And this must continue!

In this sort of climate, it may be not easy to feel like you are adapting - not to mention flourishing. Driving in a VUCA World - Leadership in the hours of Crisis is the new world order. We truly are seeing a remarkable change on the planet, and no part of our life is immaculate by this change.

From the unexpected change in our way of life to the tremendous shift in mentality, the present circumstance has constrained us all to think fast, think extraordinary, and raise versatility. Professional life is the same. In the genuine sense, the world right currently exemplifies the VUCA reasoning; Volatile, Uncertain, Complex, and Ambiguous. We were not ready for this unexpected development, and many are confused about how to adapt to this and push forward. Convenient solutions will presently don't work; this change is somewhat perpetual.

It implies that we should rethink and re-adjust every technique for activity, thinking, acting, and being. Going ahead, mental and enthusiastic well-being balance has gotten basic on an ongoing premise. The capacity to re-adjust ranges of abilities, practices, and activities according to the progressions on the planet is a consuming worry for us all.

We are affected by this in some structure or the other. What is required is Mental Health, Resilience, Self consideration and inclusivity. On the off chance that organisations and organisations are unequipped for sympathy, we can venture up and connect with companions and family members in trouble. The Covid times require that extra portion of local area administration and social awareness for sure companions. We can start a little—every single one of us. Keeping yourself propelled in any event, during the current situation where there is torment ..enduring ..passing .. lockdown.. dejection.. the world has halted. Inspiration comes from the inside.. equilibrium of the brain-body soul. In this infuriating situation, keep a quiet, adjusted, formed outlook .. keeping yourself propelled, self-inspired, and forcing others as the new practice.

"Keeping yourself roused in any event, during the current situation". Much as we like to consider these as reasonable and impartial and fearlessly take cutbacks in our step, the playing. At the point when an acquiring part loses his employment, the family's funds are seriously affected.

This is undoubtedly Sad and lamentable. The vulnerability is troubling. A few families think it's extreme to try and meet routine costs—some need to plunge into their resources. As far as strength and holding power, the family and the business are extraordinary. Like this, they need to see conservations and cutbacks with the unfortunate moments.

The individuals who have lost their positions are, in this way, taking a gander at a significant stretch of joblessness, cooped up for the most part inside their homes. Many would have managed their circumstance in protection without upsetting the family. What would we be able to do is comes a priority for all at this hour

as educators too on importance. Start Small, Start some online business. Investigate some revenue of yours as a calling. Check the old recollections to be content. Have a go at cutting your costs and requests. Be together. Efficient attempt alternatives. They search for various acquiring choices regardless of whether they are more minor or excellent. Beware of conveying on the web range of instructing/preparing/directing/the majority worldwide.

That is absolutely how I felt! As an educator. The teaching is on with no real students, in real-time physical classrooms. The learning is on but for sure at the independence of the learner. Likewise, preparation members and workshop crowds have been getting some information for quite a long time. So I chose to gather the ten best apparatuses and standards I know into a short, sharp course. Quite possibly, the most significant way to deal with flourishing in a VUCA world is the Pareto Principle, the 80:20 standard. The 80:20 principle says that you get 80% of the worth from the best 20% of the thoughts, and we end up applying it when you use it skillfully. In this way, here is the best 20%. Apply it well, and you'll have an immense effect on your prosperity at work. Learning how to learn is the new priority.

The Uncertain Times!

"There are two things we can say with conviction about the future: it will be extraordinary. Like never before, pioneers need to explore new testing times, a reviving speed of progress, expanding assumptions, and a rising

tide of quickly developing conditions. This unique and distinctive climate (VUCA) is moving pioneers to discover better approaches to lead their associations and make supported progress. Because of these conditions, there is a hunger for administration. Yet, pioneers face a tornado climate loaded with incredible freedoms and overwhelming difficulties to lead their kin and associations.

If I share the quote by Prof Sattar Bawany (2019), the Fourth Industrial Revolution (Industry 4.0) addresses a blend of Artificial Intelligence, Robotics, Cyber-Physical Systems and the Internet-of-Things (IoT). Authority 4.0 is about pioneers making their advanced change procedure and guaranteeing that it is lined up with their business's business and development plans. This is accomplished by showing successfully the set-up of next-generation initiative capabilities, which incorporate basic reasoning and imaginative speculation alongside enthusiastic and social knowledge abilities like sympathy and relationship with the board in particular.

Driving in the Fourth Industrial Revolution (Industry 4.0) spins around overseeing difficulties in a business climate that is profoundly problematic, progressively computerised and overwhelmingly unstable, *unsure, mind-boggling and vague (VUCA). Innovative headways in artificial brainpower, mechanical technology, sharing stages and the Internet of Things adjust plans of action and businesses. These progressions are occurring at an uncommon speed. Pioneers at all levels need to foster the significant capabilities and abilities to effectively adjust to new fundamental factors when driving in a troublesome VUCA World.*

VUCA is an abbreviation that arose out of the military during the 1990s. It portrays the "haze of war" — the turbulent conditions experienced in an advanced combat zone. Its importance to pioneers in business is evident, as these conditions elucidate the climate where the company is led each day. Authority, not surprisingly, including making a dream, isn't sufficient in a VUCA world. **TEACHING IN THE VUCA WORLD**, *a priority on cards,* **fetches the world of uncertainties. The new world order of VOLATILE, UNCERTAIN, COMPLEX, and AMBIGUOUS approaches reflect a new everyday learning and exploring the novel order of working.**

• Volatile: Things change eccentrically, out of nowhere, very, particularly for the more regrettable.

• *Uncertain: Important data isn't known or clear; suspicious, hazy about the current circumstance and future results; not ready to be depended upon.*

• *Complex: Many unique and associated parts: key choice factors, the connection between assorted specialists, development, variation, coevolution, feeble signs.*

• *Ambiguous: Open to more than one translation; the significance of an occasion can be perceived unexpectedly.*

Driving in a VUCA world not just gives a moving climate to pioneers to work and for chief advancement program to have an effect: it likewise gives an essential scope of new abilities. The new truth is acknowledging that new and various skills are required for pioneers to prevail in this new typical.

As educators, we need to guide our students and parents towards new destinations, which may include:

Flourish amid unpredictability, vulnerability, intricacy and equivocalness.

Recognise the need to choose what you centre around

Construct an essential organisation of essential contacts

Realise were to work at your pinnacle

Output your frame of reference for changes, patterns, dangers and openings

Bridle the basic achievement framework for life during the transition; the Powerhouse Loop

The Online Teaching and Learning with the Parents
Support

Well, finally to explore the wonders amongst the PANDEMIC and the readiness to the VUCA world, without a doubt, the word VUCA causes some cocked eyebrows and characterizes the prepared idea of shock, an evoke stun, shock, or offense, ordinarily through whimsical activities or words. The expression regularly recommends negative consideration or judgment, however my dear companions, serves a reality today.

As a head of a school, I discover checking and testing easily of solace for the educators to be locked in and module to the learning situation. The range deceives our arrangement which screens thus, training has changed drastically, with the unmistakable ascent of e-learning, whereby educating is attempted distantly and on advanced stages. The paging is organized and characterized with the characteristic of conveying the classes without any difficulty and solace of their takers.

The target of this module enacts learning concerning the Leading Change in a Pandemic VUCA World specifically. The common vision and the methodology characterizes the destinations with introduction of understanding the idea in Visualizing the learning incredibly. It incorporates about the model to deal with the world through VOCA in the COVID period. Step by step instructions to prepare pioneers to oversee through. The idea represents the Volatility, Uncertainty, Complexity, Ambiguity, as VOCA practically speaking.

Without a doubt as training suppliers, our great work is to help everybody in giving quality schooling to all even in these extraordinary occasions. The reality lies that educators will in general do twofold and surprisingly threefold the task to convey. As we as a whole scramble to adapt to the quickly evolving COVID-19 circumstance, a significant number of us are unexpectedly taking on jobs as all day guardians and substitute educators likewise with the walk for the rush to convey.

The live streaming which the guardians requested sometime in the distant past mirror the ascent of new requests and wants. What is required is the need towards conveying the exercises to give every understudy customized criticism and work on, setting them up to benefit from study hall guidance.

Happy Learning to all on priority.

Ref:
   https://www.asmaindia.in/slc-2021/speaker/dr-dheeraj-mehrotra/

VUCA CERTIFIED COURSES ONLINE

SOME UDEMY CERTIFIED COURSES ON VUCA LEARNING

Friends, as we know by now, the new ordinary proceeds with our interface Based on innovation by means of Mobile, Learning Management System (LMS), Virtual Class among other. The Mobile Segment has unquestionably come out as a main the market and will proceed so during the estimate time frame due to a consistently decrease in the gadget and web cost. VUCA is there to remain!! Let us take it as a new normal times to explore the wonders altogether.

The objective of this module activates learning with reference to the Leading Change in a Pandemic VUCA World in particular. The shared vision and the approach defines the objectives with preface of understanding the notion in Visualising the learning in a big way. It integrates about the model to manage the world through VUCA in the COVID era. How to train leaders to manage through. The concept symbolizes the Volatility, Uncertainty, Complexity, Ambiguity, as VUCA in practice.

The module defines the various formats of VUCA how at workplaces it is re-orienting the work culture and the factors which effect the pandemic era. It also focuses the priorities towards actions taken with global and local positions in preferences of uncertainty. It also shares the essential skills to lead in a VUCA world of developing a shared purpose, learning agility, self awareness, leading through collaboration and influence and gaining confidence to lead in the time of uncertainty.

Enjoy the learning guys!!

Explore via the following QR Codes Guys! Happy Learning......

Leading Change in a Pandemic VUCA World

VUCA VUCA VUCA

The world order has changed!!

The objective of this module activates learning with reference to the Leading Change in a Pandemic VUCA World in particular. The shared vision and the approach defines the objectives with preface of understanding the notion in Visualising the learning in a big way. It integrates about the model to manage the world through VUCA in the COVID era. How to train leaders to manage through. The concept symbolizes the Volatility, Uncertainty, Complexity, Ambiguity, as VUCA in practice.

The module defines the various formats of VUCA how at workplaces it is re-orienting the work culture and the factors which effect the pandemic era. It also focuses the priorities towards actions taken with global and local positions in preferences of uncertainty. It also shares the essential skills to lead in a VUCA world of developing a shared purpose, learning agility, self awareness, leading through collaboration and influence and gaining confidence to lead in the time of uncertainty.

Learn to live in a VUCA world

Dr. Dheeraj Mehrotra is an Author, Teacher Trainer, School Auditor, A National Teacher Awardee, engaged as a Principal at NPS International School, Guwahati, Assam. He has authored over 80 plus books on various topics and has also been listed in the LIMCA Book of records and INDIA Book of Records for his innovation in Education. As a TEDx speaker and as a premium UDEMY Instructor he has also developed over 400 Courses and believes in learning to learn as a priority. He can be visited at www.authordheerajmehrotra.com

Books By The Same Author

Use the following QR Code to explore the books!

Happy Reading!

www.ingramcontent.com/pod-product-compliance
Lightning Source LLC
Chambersburg PA
CBHW070233260726
48658CB00006BA/2312